# USER GROUPS IN SPORT

## PEOPLE WITH DISABILITIES
- Or ability!
- Now far higher profile after London 2012 (at least at elite level).
- Sport England increasing funding for clubs to be more inclusive. (more on page 13).
- Disabilities may be wide & varied. Not all can be seen. Examples include: wheelchair users, amputees, deaf/blind, people with learning difficulties.

## UNEMPLOYED OR ECONOMICALLY DISADVANTAGED
- Socio-economic is a huge factor.
- People may be 'time rich' but 'monetarily poor'.
- Unemployed - no job. Disadvantaged - low paid job & re ups, such as Uni.
- Many families reliant on food banks - Aug 2.17 million people.
- May get worse w/ high inflation.
- Therefore a lack income to afford sport/exercise.

## PARENTS
- Single or couples.
- People with children.
- have huge constraints on time to play sport/exercise, especially if they work.
- Exercise with children?
- Exercise while their child is at football/netball/ who looks after children?

## PEOPLE WHO WORK
- May have to fit sports & exercise around their job.
- eg swim in the morning before work, or run after.
- Many may be able to alter their commute eg run or cycle.
- More flexibility now post-Covid - working from home.
- People may go to the gym or a walk at lunch time.

## PEOPLE WITH FAMILY COMMITMENTS
- Usually a regular event weekly/monthly. Examples may include...
- taking your kids to dance class at the weekend, football/cricket practice midweek.
- Having family over for Sunday dinner.
- Limits 'leisure time' or available time for sport.

## YOUNG CHILDREN
- For the purpose of this exam this means 'birth to the end of Primary School'.

## TEENAGERS
- For the purpose of this exam this means compulsory secondary school age.' Pressure of exams!
- Issues very similar. A lack of free/leisure time for sport as at school daily (except holidays).
- Reliant on parents to transport to/from games & training.
- Reliant on parents to cover cost of memberships & equipment. Can be expensive. eg. golf.

# POSSIBLE BARRIERS

**ALL** these factors link in with the user groups found on pages 1 & 2.

## LACK OF DISPOSABLE INCOME

- Plays a very big role in participation.
- Links with employment & unemployment.
- Big issue currently due to 40 year high inflation & below inflation pay increases.
- People with low levels of disposable income will not be able to afford to play golf, go skiing or horseriding.
- May go running or play football as are cheaper/require less equipment.

## LACK OF SPORTING ROLE MODELS

- More of an issue for certain user groups than others. e.g. disabled, ethnic minorities, women.
- Very important, children want to emulate their heroes. e.g. England Lionesses winning football Euro 2022 - will it inspire new generation?
- Very few British Asian footballers. Most recent e.g. Zidane Iqbal at Manchester United.

## FAMILY COMMITMENTS

- May leave a lack of free time / leisure time for sport & exercise.
- e.g. taking young children to clubs, caring for a parent or helping elderly grandparents with appointments.

## LACK OF TRANSPORT

- May link to a lack of disposable income; unable to afford a car (+ upkeep, insurance & petrol), or public transport.
- This severely limits access to clubs. Have to be within walking distance.
- Less of a problem in urban areas, more of an issue in remote areas e.g. countryside (infrequent public transport).

## EMPLOYMENT & UNEMPLOYMENT

- People in work (employed) may be able to afford to play sport, join a gym, afford sports equipment, but may not have much 'leisure time' to do so.
- Unemployed people (without a job) may have the time to be active & exercise, but cannot afford to join a gym, play sport & buy sports equipment. They have very limited 'disposable income.'
- Some councils offer discounts on council run leisure centres, swimming pools & tennis courts. e.g. Brighton - 40% discount on a 6 month pass. Better Living run over 100 facilities across the United Kingdom & Northern Ireland & offer discounted off-peak memberships.

## LEISURE TIME
- time when not working or occupied. 'Free time.'

## DISPOSABLE INCOME
- income after taxes have been deducted & essential bills have been paid.

# CONTENTS

**Topic Area 1: Issues which affect participation in sport**

1. User groups in sport.
2. User groups in sport.
3. Possible barriers.
4. Possible barriers.
5. Possible solutions to barriers affecting participation.
6. Possible solutions to barriers affecting participation.
7. Factors impacting the popularity of sport in the UK.
8. Factors impacting the popularity of sport in the UK.
9. Sport in the UK.

**Topic Area 2: The role of sport in promoting values**

10. Values promoted through sport
11. The Olympics and Paralympics.
12. Initiatives.
13. Initiatives.
14. Etiquette & sporting behaviour.
15. Performance Enhancing Drugs.
16. The World Anti-Doping Agency: WADA
17. Performance Enhancing Drugs.

**Topic Area 3: The implications of hosting a major sporting event for a city or country**

18. Major sporting events.
19. Hosting a major sporting event - pre event impacts.
20. Potential positive benefits during the event.
21. Potential negative aspects during the event.
22. Post event benefits.
23. Post event drawbacks.

**Topic Area 4: The role National Governing Bodies (NGBs) play in the development of their sport.**

24. National Governing Bodies.
25. National Governing Bodies.

**Topic Area 5: The use of technology in sport**

26. Technology in sport.
27. Technology in sport.
28. Technology in sport.
29. Contemporary technologies.
30. The impact of technology.
31. Contemporary recovery methods.
32. Technology in sport.

Plus

33. Extended writing Questions.
34. Notes.
35. Notes.

# USER GROUPS IN SPORT

There are many different user groups in sport. You need to learn all these...

- **GENDER**
- **DIFFERENT ETHNIC GROUPS**
- **RETIRED/OVER 60s**
- **FAMILIES WITH CHILDREN**
- **CARERS**
- **PEOPLE WITH FAMILY COMMITMENTS**
- **YOUNG CHILDREN**
- **TEENAGERS**
- **DISABLED**
- **PARENTS**
- **WORKING PEOPLE**
- **UNEMPLOYED**

## GENDER
- Most sports now played by both sexes. e.g. football, rugby.
- Adult versions played against own sex. Football can be mixed up to U18s.
- Mixed doubles common e.g. badminton, tennis.
- New mixed relays in swimming & athletics.
- Transgenders - very big/hot topic currently. Many NGBs currently banning trans-gender women competing (unfair advantage?) e.g. FINA, UCI, RFU, RFL.
- New 'open' category in the future?

## PEOPLE FROM DIFFERENT ETHNIC GROUPS
- Religion & culture can have a huge impact on sports played. e.g. Cricket is huge amongst the Indian & Pakistani communities.
- Many Muslims attend daily Mosque, so limited 'leisure time'.
- Muslims (some) Jewish women unable to attend mixed sex sessions e.g. swimming.
- Racist abuse still aimed at Black footballers. (Euro 2020).

## FAMILIES WITH CHILDREN
- Main issue here is balancing work/family commitments with sport/activity.
- Does the leisure facility have a crèche. Childcare may be an issue.
- Traditionally the woman is still seen as the homemaker.
- Active Parents = Active kids. Take part together.

## CARERS
- Can be any age/sex.
- Generally look after a member of their family (parent, sibling) instead of hired/paid help.
- Limited 'leisure time' because of this (job on top?), though sport may provide an escape/break.

## RETIRED/OVER 60s
- The social aspect of sport is very important. Meet friends to play/exercise.
- More 'leisure time' as not working, however most may have less 'disposable income' as reliant on pension (state and/or private) for money.
- Stereotype activities include bowls, golf & tennis.
- Longer to recover from injuries sustained (due to age).

# POSSIBLE BARRIERS

## THE LACK OF EQUAL COVERAGE IN THE MEDIA - FOCUSSED ON...

**GENDER**
**ETHNICITY**

- There has been a 'male bias' of media coverage for years. Most popular sports covered are football, rugby & horse racing.
- More male sports reporters/pundits, though this is now changing, eg. Gabby Logan, Alex Scott, Karen Carney amongst others.
- Increased coverage of WSL 2021/22 on BBC & Sky. Impact? Increased participation. All Euro 2022 games on BBC for the Lionesses' victory. Most watched in 2022 final - so far 17.4 million & 5.9 million streamed on BBC iPlayer.
- Very few Ethnic Minority role models focussed on in sport. Currently Dina Asher-Smith/Athletics. Less focus in main stream media.
- Very few British Asian footballers. Most recent eg. Zidane Iqbal at Manchester United.

## REMEMBER

- All these possible barriers which affect participation in sport link to USER **GROUPS**.
- Some barriers may impact more than one user group. eg appropriate provision may impact multiple groups.

## LACK OF POSITIVE FAMILY ROLE MODELS OR FAMILY SUPPORT

- Can influence participation in a positive or negative way.
- Active Parents = Active kids.
- Children likely to participate in sports/activities their parents are involved in. eg. cricket, cycling, netball - play the same sport (maybe together?)
- Parents take children to clubs... or may not have time to (due to work/other family commitments).

## LACK OF APPROPRIATE ACTIVITY PROVISION

- Are the activities in a certain town/city/area suitable for the **USERS**. If not this will limit participation.
- Can be impacted by...
- Cost - may be too expensive for some.
- Locality - some may not be able to travel.
- Time - may be at work/school.

## LACK OF AWARENESS...

- of appropriate activity provision.
- People may not know what activities are running & where.
- How do you find out now? Generally online/social media.
- This may disproportionally affect some groups. eg. **OVER 60s**, **UNEMPLOYED**.

# Possible Solutions to Barriers Affecting Participation

## Potential Solutions...
Think **PAP**
- **P**rovision
- **A**ppropriate **A**ccess
- **P**romotion

## PROMOTION STRATEGIES

### TARGETED
- Letting specific groups know what is available for them.
- Could be local/national newspapers, radio, local TV, buses, leaflets.
- Increases visibility & helps combat lack of awareness.
- Special offers, incentives.

### ROLE MODELS
- Again could be local/national level.
- Athletes/performers used to target specific groups eg - Women, Ethnic Minorities.
- Aim to increase the number of participants in specific user groups.
- Role models can be used to front...

### INITIATIVES
- Have the aim of increasing participation amongst specific user groups.
- More on pages
- Can be local/national
- eg - Reduced price membership for the unemployed, free hot drinks for the over 60's (local) or #ThisGirlCan (national).

## PROVISION of...

### APPROPRIATE PROGRAMMES AND SESSIONS
- Different ages/user groups have different needs & wants.
- Having appropriate activities on at the right place (& right time - see below) is vital to gain traction with users.
- eg - Women only swim times, day time slots aimed at parents with young children (have a crèche available), specific slots for OAPs, disabled, wheelchair users will increase usage.
- Evening/weekend slots for league events - high usage.

### APPROPRIATE ACTIVITIES
- Again different ages/user groups have different wants & needs.
- eg - In a leisure centre, have a range of classes to accommodate everyone! Yoga, Pilates, Zumba, Body Pump, HIIT, Spinning, Low Impact (for OAPs/60's).
- Multi-use sportshall - flexibility.

### TIMES
- Links with appropriate programmes & sessions.
- The programme must reflect times when user groups can attend.
- eg - OAPs - during day, working population - after 4-5pm, shiftworkers - daytime, young children & teenagers 4-6pm.

# POSSIBLE SOLUTIONS TO BARRIERS AFFECTING PARTICIPATION

## AVAILABILITY OF APPROPRIATE USER GROUP FACILITIES AND EQUIPMENT

- Again, this is another key driver in allowing as many user groups as possible the opportunity to participate.
- Does a leisure centre have a small separate pool for young children/families to learn to swim?
- Does the main pool have a hoist to allow access for wheelchair users?
- Adapted equipment such as hand cycles in the gym, boccia & indoor curling would allow more disabled people appropriate opportunities.
- Are signs/information available in braille for blind/partially sighted & hearing loops for people who use hearing aids?

### REMEMBER:
- Some user groups may be disproportionately affected by barriers!

## IMPROVED ACCESS TO FACILITIES FOR ALL USERS

- This avoids certain groups being discriminated against.
- eg. women only swim times, availability of crèche facilities, sessions for children after school, ramps, wider doors, rails, accessible changing for people with mobility issues.

## INCREASED AND APPROPRIATE TRANSPORT AVAILABILITY

- The availability of appropriate transport links to & from a sports club/leisure facility is a huge factor that may limit participation.
- Many user groups may not have access to a car. eg. Unemployed, children, over 60s etc.
- Therefore reliant on public transport.
- There has been a 16% decline in bus services in 2020/21. More cuts forecast (Post-Pandemic).
- Local authorities in England & Wales cut £182 million from subsidised bus routes in the past decade (2010-2020), affecting 3,000 routes.
- Could clubs/leisure facilities offer a free/subsidised bus collection service for users in an attempt to boost usage?

## APPROPRIATE PRICING FOR ALL USER GROUPS

- Again avoids discrimination.
- Lots of ways to do this.
- Offer reduced/concessionary prices/memberships for those on low incomes, free for under 5s, special rates for teenagers or the over 60s, cheaper rates during the 'working' day.

# Factors Impacting the Popularity of Sports in the UK

These factors can be...
- POSITIVE
- NEGATIVE

There are 8 you need to know... Remember...

**REPS & MAPS**
- **R**ole Models
- **E**nvironment/Climate
- **P**articipants
- **S**pectator Opportunities
- **M**edia Coverage
- **A**cceptability (Social)
- **P**rovision
- **S**uccess

## Role Models
- Positive role models can drive participation in sport.
- eg. Adam Peaty (swimming), Max Whitlock (gymnastics), Dina Asher-Smith (athletics), Ella Toone (women's football), David Weir (Para-athletics).
- Some groups are under-represented - eg disabled, women, ethnic minorities, over 60s. This lack of role models can inhibit participation.
- People, especially children want to emulate/copy their role models.
- Vital they set a good example.
- Negative behaviours may also be copied if seen live/on TV.

## Environment/Climate
- Plays a huge role in which sports/activities you can participate in.
- Near the outdoors? eg - the Lake District / Peak District. Access to walking, rock climbing, sailing, ghyll scrambling.
- Limited access to winter sports, unless you live in the Highlands of Scotland eg skiing, snowboarding. Have to travel abroad. Huge cost implications. Only 6 indoor slopes in the UK.
- Britain has a temperate climate - good for most games (winter) & summer sports.

## Participants
- Covid has played a large role in impacting the rate of participation in sport.
- There has been a clear fall in activity levels compared to pre-pandemic (Nov 18-19).
- More on the most recent Active Lives survey on page 9.

## Live Spectator Opportunities
- Physically going to a game, visiting a stadium to watch.
- Again numbers hugely affected by Covid (20-21), but have bounced back.
- Record attendance at Wembley for Women's Euro 2022 final 87,192 - more than men's final!
- Opportunities to watch NFL & NBA games in London.

# FACTORS IMPACTING THE POPULARITY OF SPORTS IN THE UK

## PROVISION OF FACILITIES
- Varies widely across the country, depending on the area, eg inner city, rural.
- There are thousands of grass football pitches, but less than 560 3G astroturf pitches.
- Lack of access for many sports, such as tennis courts, ice rinks.
- Increase in number of Play Parks & Outdoor Fitness Equipment.

## HIGH LEVEL SUCCESS
- of both individuals & teams... & countries
- Creates role models.
- Knock on effect is an increase in participation.
- eg Chris Hoy, Jason Kenny in cycling in the Olympics (13 golds). Chris Froome's Tour de France successes. Eve Muirhead & team winning Olympic gold in curling. England's women's team winning football Euro 2022.

## SOCIAL ACCEPTABILITY
- Has been a debate around boxing for many years. Now also UFC/MMA (violence).
- Recently allowed female fights.
- Horse Racing - animal cruelty with use of whip.
- 2016 - Muirfield (golf) lost the Open as no female members were allowed.

## MEDIA COVERAGE
- Focussed on the range & amount.
- Sport & the media have a very symbiotic relationship.
- The globalisation of sport has led to extensive media coverage. eg Euro 2020 on both BBC & ITV, Euro 2022 (women's) all games covered by the BBC for the first time.
- Fan bases for major sports reach far & wide.

### TYPES OF MEDIA
- **TV** - live, highlights, catch up - eg BBC iPlayer. Can be Terrestrial eg BBC, ITV or Satellite eg Sky, BT, Virgin media. These outlets offer sports packages that can be tailored to the viewer. Sky Sports - channels for
  - football
  - golf
  - cricket
  - formula 1.
- **RADIO** - live commentaries. cheaper than TV eg 5Live
- **INTERNET** - streaming live events eg YouTube.

## NEWSPAPERS
- broadsheets (factual), tabloids (sensationalise). Tabloids more sports coverage.

### PAY PER VIEW
- relatively new. Viewers pay a fee for a special event/programme. Mainly used for Boxing & UFC.

### CLUB CHANNEL
- some big clubs have their own channel. eg Man United - MUTV.

# SPORT IN THE UK

## Useful websites to use...
- www.sportengland.org
- www.youthsporttrust.org
- www.yksport.gov.uk
- www.thefa.com
- www.englandnetball.co.uk
- www.englandrugby.com

## SPORT ENGLAND
- Run 2 Active Lives surveys
  - Adults
  - Children.
- Measures the nation's activity levels.
- Results from the Adult Nov 20/21 survey show...
- *These results include the covid lockdown period.
- 27.2% of people (12.4m) do less than 30mins activity per week
- 11.5% of people (5.2m) are fairly active, but less than 150 mins activity per week.
- 61.4% of people (28.0m) did an average of 150 mins activity per week.

## GENDER
- Men (63%, 14.0m) more likely to be active than women (60%, 13.9m).

## MOST POPULAR ACTIVITIES
- Walking for leisure - 24m ↑
- Active travel (wal./cycle) - 11.9m ↓
- Fitness activities - 11.4m ↓
- Running - 6.2m
- Cycling (for leisure) - 6.5m ↑
- Swimming - 2.0m
- Team sports - 2.2m ↑
- *from 18/19 survey

## SOCIO-ECONOMIC
- Workers (71% active), compared to unemployed (52% active).

## DISABILITY
- No disability (66% active) compared to disabled/long term health conditions (45% active).

## ETHNICITY
- differences based on background. White British (63%), Black (55%), Asian (50%).

## EMERGING / NEW SPORTS
- This is an ever changing picture.
- Recently, activities such as ultimate frisbee, girls rugby & HIIT training (high intensity interval training) have become more popular.
- What next? New/ emerging sports include...

**KINBALL** - 3 teams at once, 1 very large ball played indoors. Keep off floor.

**FOOTGOLF** - a 'hybrid' combining football & golf. Kick a football into a hole - like golf.

**EXTREME RUNNING** - run across tough courses & trails. eg- Colour Runs, Tough Mudder.

**DISC GOLF** - similar to golf, but played with a 'disc' (frisbee). The disc is thrown at a target.

**QUIDDITCH** - based 'loosely' on the game in the Harry Potter films, it is a combination of tag, rugby & dodgeball.

# VALUES PROMOTED THROUGH SPORT

## CITIZENSHIP
- Working with others in sport in your LOCAL area helps create & develop community links & volunteering spirit. e.g. volunteering at a local grassroots rugby or netball club.
- This may be as a volunteer coach, play leader, first aider or steward.

## TOLERANCE & RESPECT
- Sport allows an athlete or performer to develop a greater understanding of other cultures & values.
- e.g. Muslim footballers fasting & playing during Ramadan.
- One value, not two!

## INCLUSION
- Sport can be used as a vehicle to unite communities & get under-represented social groups active & involved.
- e.g. Ethnic Minorities, Women, OAPs

## TEAM SPIRIT
- 'Teamwork', working effectively with others, supporting team mates.
- Co-operate to collectively achieve a common good. i.e. win a game!
- Players have a sense of belonging & develop friendships within their team/club.

## EXCELLENCE
- Can be seen at any level! Non-league to international, an athlete/performer should always strive to be the 'best they can be!'
- Work with maximum effort levels... always!
- This is one of the OLYMPIC VALUES (see page 11).

## FAIR PLAY
- Plays with SPORTSMANSHIP!
- Players stick to the rules of the game, both written & unwritten.
- Players display good sporting etiquette.
- National Governing Bodies (NGBs) now promote this.
- e.g. the FIFA Fair Play Award.
- Players/athletes want to win, but 'not at all costs!'

## NATIONAL PRIDE
- Major sporting events can develop a feeling of 'national pride' towards a team/athlete/sport.
- e.g. the London Olympics in 2012, the Women's Football Euro 2022 Lionesses' win!
- The country unites behind the team/athlete/sport, willing them to succeed.

# THE OLYMPICS AND PARALYMPICS

## THE OLYMPIC SYMBOL/FLAG
- Has a white background & 5 interlocking rings.
- This represents the 5 continents & the closeness between them.
- The 6 colours (including white) appear at least once on each national flag.

## THE FIRST GAMES
1896 in Athens. 5 days, 9 sports, 32 events, 13 countries, 311 athletes... but no women. That was in Paris in 1900.

## OLYMPIC VALUES
**EXCELLENCE** - strive to do your best both in sport & life. Taking part not winning, making progress & enjoying a healthy body, will & mind.

**RESPECT** - yourself, your body, others, rules, officials, the sport & the environment.

**FRIENDSHIP** - at the core of the Olympic Movement/Olympism. Sport is a vehicle to develop an understanding of others, their beliefs & cultures.

## PARALYMPIC VALUES
- First held in Rome in 1960.

**COURAGE** - encompasses the unique spirit of the Paralympic athlete.

**DETERMINATION** - Paralympic athletes push themselves to the limit... and beyond!

**INSPIRATION** - from the stories & achievements of Paralympic athletes. Role models.

**EQUALITY** - Paralympic sport helps breakdown social barriers for people with impairments.

## PIERRE DE COUBERTIN

- Baron Pierre de Coubertin can be credited as the founder of the modern day Olympic movement.
- He developed the ideals surrounding the modern Olympic Games.
- De Coubertin wanted to 'revive' the ancient Olympic Games ideal & inspired by the Much Wenlock Games in Shropshire, set about doing so.
- the aim of Olympism was to foster better relationships through sport.

## THE OLYMPIC CREED

- Learn this! It has regularly been on previous exams... fill in the missing words.
- It has been on the score board during the opening ceremony at every modern Olympic Games.

'The most important thing is not to win but to take part, just as the most important thing in life is not the triumph, but the struggle. The essential thing is not to have conquered, but to have fought well.' - Pierre de Coubertin.

# INITIATIVES

## WHAT ARE THEY?

**INITIATIVES** – strategies or campaigns put together by National Governing Bodies (NGBs), or Sports Organisations (Sport England) to target certain user groups in an effort to increase participation. This may be due to barriers they face.

## INITIATIVES

- Can link in with values promoted through sport (as seen on page 10) include...
  - TEAM SPIRIT
  - FAIR PLAY
  - CITIZENSHIP
  - TOLERANCE AND RESPECT
  - INCLUSION
  - NATIONAL PRIDE
  - EXCELLENCE

- There are many, many examples of local, regional & national campaigns covered on the next page.

- You should learn the differences between them & what the initiative/campaigns are hoping to achieve. i.e. WHAT are the aims.

- They are all looking to increase participation rates in specific user groups, but are they looking to improve wellbeing, mental health, self-esteem, employability etc.

## INITIATIVES can be...
- LOCAL
- REGIONAL
- NATIONAL

### LOCAL
- The initiative, campaign or event is focussed on a specific town or city to breakdown barriers for specific user groups.
- eg. Liverpool Lifestyles is offering free swimming for under 16s during the summer holidays (2022).

### REGIONAL
- The initiative, campaign or event is focussed on a wider scale, such as a county or area eg. Lancashire or the North West.
- eg. Greater Manchester Moving is a programme across all 12 boroughs of Greater Manchester with a focus on 3 key user groups
  - Children & young people
  - People out of work
  - People with long term health conditions.
- The aim is to improve activity rates on a large scale in a sustainable manner.

### NATIONAL
- The initiative, campaign or event is focussed on the whole country eg. England.
- It may be driven by Sport England, the Youth Sport Trust or the Government.
- eg. #ThisGirlCan - a national campaign celebrating active women, whatever their sport, level, '... no matter how well they do, how they look or even how red their face.'
- A TV & social media campaign to increase activity rates/levels in women.

# INITIATIVES

## BREAKING BOUNDARIES
- Aim - to socially connect young people, families & communities together through regular cricket engagement.
- Delivered in 5 cities... Bradford, Birmingham, Manchester, Slough & London.

## The Youth Sport Trust
The Youth Sport Trust along with Sport England implement numerous initiatives & programmes that target certain groups who may be unable to access sport and/or physical activity, including...

- Both YST & Sport England are actively involved in funding & introducing programmes to encourage participation for the population & target groups.

## ACTIVE ACROSS AGES
- Developed as a pilot project to improve the physical, mental & social wellbeing of participants, provide volunteering opportunities, develop employability skills/confidence & to be physically active.
- Also provides opportunities to support primary to secondary transition & enhance local community relationships between young people & older adults.

## SAINSBURY'S ACTIVE KIDS FOR ALL INCLUSIVE PE TRAINING
- Provides training & resources to support teachers, trainees & school staff to provide high quality PE lessons for children.

## SCHOOL GAMES
- Funded by Sport England, delivered by YST, the School Games started in 2006 as a single annual multi-sport competition, with a National Final.
- In 2010, it was expanded to include more localised competitions, with major county events to smaller competitions within the same school.

## GIRLS ACTIVE
- Aim - to improve girls attitudes towards PE, increase participation in PE & sport, improve self-esteem & confidence and to improve school-student relationships in PE & across the school.

## BOYS MOVE
- An approach that addresses the wellbeing challenges of working class boys through PE & sport.

## BEE WELL
- To be rolled out across secondary schools in Greater Manchester for 3 years (Autumn 2021). Aim to improve wellbeing of young people.

# ETIQUETTE AND SPORTING BEHAVIOUR

## WHY?
- Allows for games where no-one is seeking an unfair advantage.
- Promotes the value of **fairplay**
- Creates a safe playing environment.

## ETIQUETTE
- Is an unwritten rule, not usually enforced, but observed. It is the way sportsmen/women behave (in a positive manner). **SPORTSMANSHIP** reinforces the value & safety for participants within games/activities.

## SPORTSMANSHIP
- 'Play & abide by the rules, win & lose graciously.'
- Sportsmen & women are **role models** & should play & adhere to the written (& unwritten) rules of the sport.
- **Fair play**, being **respectful** & **polite** behaviour are all important.
- eg. shaking hands at the end of the game (win, lose or draw). Helping an injured opponent.

## SPECTATOR ETIQUETTE
- As with the players/performers, it is **watching in a respectful manner.**
- eg. being quiet during the opposing national anthem during rallies & serves in tennis, place kicks in rugby & tee shots in golf.
- Fans can create a great atmosphere. eg. midweek European Cup matches - noise, chanting, singing.
- Give the **home team** an **advantage**; boo, whistle, jeers opposition.
- However, can also have a negative effect...
- Potential for crowd trouble and hooliganism inside/outside the ground.
- Safety concerns - costly! Police, stewards & CCTV.

## SPORTSMANSHIP
- Creates positive role models (for children)
- Displays the sport in a positive light.
- Sets good example.

## GAMESMANSHIP
- Creates poor role models.
- Displays the sport in a negative light.
- Sets a bad example.

## GAMESMANSHIP
- The use of dubious though not illegal methods to win or gain an advantage.
- 'Bending the rules, not breaking them!'
- All done with the intention of winning.
- eg. Timewasting in football. Sledging in cricket to get a psychological advantage. Diving in football after a tackle to influence the ref to give a free kick... or is that **DEVIANCE?**

# Performance Enhancing Drugs

## Drug Use...

- To **enhance performance** has been a problem in sport for a long time.
- There is evidence that PEDs were used in **Ancient Greek times**, with athletes using hallucinogenic mushrooms, sesame seeds & brandy/wine mixtures to enhance performance.
- In the current climate, PEDs have become a **lucrative source of income** on the black market.
- As the technology surrounding PEDs ever increases, so too does the technology for testing to catch drug cheats (see page 16).

## Why Take Them?

- Enhances performance, with increased chance of success. Success = wealth & fame.
- Think others doing so, creates level playing field.
- Decreases recovery time, train harder for longer.
- Pressure? From coach, sponsor.
- Need to succeed.
- 'Win at all costs' attitude.
- Stress of competition.
- Lack of moral compass. Why not?

## Examples of PED Use

Includes...
- Racehorses in the 1900s were given substances to increase their speed.
- The Soviet & East German state funded doping regime post WWII was at it's height in the 1970s & 80s. The idea was to show the successes of the Communist state.
- In 1988, one of the biggest drug taking scandals occurred at the Seoul Olympics, with the winner of the men's 100m final (**Ben Johnson** of Canada) testing positive for Stanozolol - an Anabolic steroid.
- **Tyson Gay** failed 3 drugs tests in quick succession in 2012 & as a result lost the medals he won at the London Olympics.
- After an IOC investigation, it was concluded that **Russia** ran a state sponsored doping programme from 2011 & have been banned from all major international events since 2016.
- In 2012 **WADA** stripped **Lance Armstrong** of all his victories, including his record 7 Tour de France titles (1999-2005) for **Blood Doping** (see page 17).

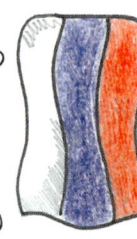

## Why Not Take Them

- Poor role model.
- Lose records, medals and sponsorship deals.
- It is immoral & is cheating/illegal.
- Long term health risks.
- Gives sport a bad name. e.g. cycling, athletics.
- Lose respect, career potentially ruined.
- Fines - up to $1 million, depending on severity.
- Loss of spectators, don't want to watch cheats!

# THE WORLD ANTI-DOPING AGENCY: WADA

## THE ROLE OF WADA

- Founded in 1999, an International Independent Agency, funded by the sports movement and national governments.
- WADA aims to bring consistency to anti-doping policies & regulations within sports organisations & governments worldwide.
- Leads a collaborative worldwide movement for 'doping free' sport.
- Plays the lead role in scientific, research, education & developing anti-doping capabilities & monitoring.
  (World Anti-Doping Code).
- Governments, International Governing Bodies (eg FIFA) & National Governing Bodies (eg the RFU) agree to this code & sign up as signatories.
- Within WADA, there is an intelligence & investigation team that work with law enforcement to target & shut down large scale doping rings.

## DRUG TESTING

- First occurred in the 1960 Athletics Championships in Budapest, then 2 years later at the 1968 Olympics in Mexico City.
- A sample tests positive, test the B sample.
- B sample positive = BAN!
- 1st offence = 4 years ...if the athlete deliberately cheated!
- Otherwise - 2 years (no fault/negligence).
- Multiple Anti-Doping rule violations or the presence of multiple substances can lead to the sanction being increased - 4 + years.

## HUNT DOWN

The drugs cheats. Test...
- HAIR
- URINE
- NAILS
- TESTING BLOOD

## EDUCATIONAL STRATEGIES

- Key to 'beating' drug cheats.
- The World Anti-Doping Code (2021) has a big focus on education & the negative impact of drug use.
- UK Anti-Doping Campaign 100% me. #BeSqueaky clean sport stud.
- Use clean athletes & peers to promote.

## WHEREABOUTS RULE

- Introduced in 2004.
- Athletes must provide to their Anti-Doping Agency (eg UK Anti-Doping) details of their location for one hour everyday between 5am & 11pm.
- 2015 - standard 2 years ban for missing 3 in 12 months.
- eg- Christian Coleman (American sprinter) had a 2 year ban reduced to 18 months for missing 3 tests in 2019.

# Performance Enhancing Drugs

## INCLUDE
- Anabolic Steroids
- Beta Blockers
- Diuretics
- Stimulants
- Peptide Hormones
- Narcotic Analgesics

Plus
- Blood Doping (A Process)

## Anabolic Steroids
- Mimics testosterone.
- Most widely available & commonly used.
- Increases muscle mass, strength & power.
- Increases the ability to train harder for longer, with a decrease in rest time between sessions.
- eg - Stanozolol, Nandrolone.
- **Benefits** - Sprinters, Boxers, Weightlifters, Rugby players (Power athletes).
- **Side Effects** - loads!! liver damage, infertility, moodiness, aggression, CHD. Addictive.

## Narcotic Analgesics
- 'painkillers' 'mask injury' from overtraining or impact. Can make it worse. Can compete when injured. eg Morphine, Heroin.
- **Benefits** - any injured athlete
- **Side Effects** - Highly addictive, depression, anxiety, lack of focus.

## Beta Blockers
- Reduces the muscle tension & BP.
- Decrease effect of adrenaline.
- Improve fine motor control & precise movements. From doctor.
- **Benefits** - Archery, Shooting.
- **Side Effects** - Nausea, heart problems, tiredness/weakness. Less $O_2$ delivery.

## Peptide Hormones
- eg - HGH & EPO
  - HGH - Human Growth Hormone.
  - EPO - Erythropoietin.
- Naturally occurring in the body
- HGH - increases muscle mass (similar to anabolic steroids) &
- EPO - increases RBC production - effect - more $O_2$ to working muscles (capacity).
- **Benefits** - EPO - endurance athletes, HGH - power athletes.
- **Side Effects** - HGH - heart failure, abnormal hand/foot growth. EPO - thicker blood, clots.

## Diuretics
- 'masking agent'. Can flush other drugs out. Weight loss → speeds up urine production → lose excess fluids.
- **Benefits** - anyone that needs to make a weight category eg Boxers, Jockeys.
- **Side Effects** - dehydration, kidney damage, nausea, headaches.

## Stimulants
- Increases alertness, reactions & aggression. Increases HR so more $O_2$ to working muscles. Impacts Central Nervous System.
- eg - caffeine, amphetamines.
- **Benefits** - Sprinters, Boxers, Cyclists.
- **Side Effects** - High blood pressure, increased HR, insomnia.

## Blood Doping
- Not the use of PEDs, but a process.
- Refers to the injection of oxygen rich blood into an athlete in an illegal attempt to boost performance.
- Can give a 20% improvement in carrying $O_2$ to working muscles.
- **Benefits** - Endurance athletes. eg Runners, cyclists.
- **Side Effects** - infection from equipment, (HIV, hepatitis), thicker blood viscosity, clots.

# MAJOR SPORTING EVENTS

The type & scheduling of major sporting events can be...
- REGULAR
- ONE-OFF
- REGULAR & RECURRING

## REGULAR

- As the name suggests, this is a _regular_ event that is held at roughly the same time each year, but in a different city/country. The host city may be 're-visited' every few years.

eg. the Champions League & Europa League Finals (football).

The Open (golf) has 14 venues that can host, of which 10 are currently in a rota to be used.

## REGULAR & RECURRING

- As the name suggests, this is a _regular_ event, held at roughly the same time each year in the _same place_ (host city).

eg. the FA Cup at Wembley.
the British Grand Prix at Silverstone.
the Challenge Cup (rugby league) at Wembley.
Wimbledon Tennis Championship.

## 'ONE-OFF'

- Usually held 'one-off' / very infrequently.
- Usually 'Quadrennial' - every _4 years_, but can be 'Biennial' - every _2 years_.

eg. the World Athletic Championships.

- Examples include... the Olympics, Commonwealth Games, Football, Rugby & Cricket World Cups

eg. London has hosted the Summer Olympics in 1908, 1948 & 2012.

## NATURE OF SPECTATORS

- 'One-off' events will attract fans from the countries of the teams/athletes competing.
- This is also true for 'Regular' & 'Regular and Recurring' events.
- The impact of this is huge! £$ - ticket sales, fans
- Revenue from travelling, staying in hotels, tourism, spending money in shops.

Direct - coming to watch games.
Indirect - travelling afterwards.

## NATURE OF PARTICIPANTS

All 3 types of events have competitors from various countries.
Impact - attracts a potentially huge global audience.
eg. Tokyo 2020 (2021) Olympics.

# HOSTING A MAJOR SPORTING EVENT - PRE EVENT IMPACTS

There can be both
- **Positive**
- **NEGATIVE**

impacts of hosting a major sporting event. These include...

## BIDDING

- Is expensive and you may not win!! It cost the Government & the British Olympic Association (BoA) £17 million between 2003-2005.
- Tokyo failed in their bid to host the 2016 Olympics, spending almost $150 million! Their successful 2020 bid cost $75 million.
- The process is open to bribery, as with the Football World Cup bids of Russia (2018) & Qatar (2022). Allegations of monetary bribes to voting confederations.
- Reputational damage for the host city/country if unsuccessful.
- Conversely, if the bid is successful, it can raise the profile of the city/country, laying the platform for increased commercialism, investment, tourism and an increase in national/local pride.

## DEVELOPING INFRASTRUCTURE AND TRANSPORT SYSTEMS

- Needs forward planning & investment.
- Roads, rail, housing/hotels, energy supply.
- For both athletes & visitors
- Expensive!
- Though will be beneficial afterwards. eg London 2012 - new Javelin High Speed Train into Central London.

## INCREASED EMPLOYMENT

- Though this may be short lived before/during the event.
- Construction of stadia & infrastructure before the event, hospitality during.
- However, after the event these jobs disappear.
- Workers may be migrants, issues re conditions eg Qatar 2022. It is estimated 6500 workers (& counting) have died in the lead 10 years (since they won the hosting rights).

## FINANCIAL/COMMERCIAL INVESTMENT
- attracts money & big companies to the host city/country. Can benefit socially/economically.
This may come from business to build stadia/infrastructure or TV rights. However, taxes may increase to pay for this.

## LOCAL/NATIONAL OBJECTIONS - Cost to taxpayer!
Money spent better elsewhere? eg. schools, social housing. What about the rest of the country?

19

# Potential Positive Benefits During the Event

## GREATER NATIONAL INTEREST IN SPORT
- Often spoken as the 'legacy' effect.
- Increased participation, role models created, grassroots programmes as well as elite programmes develop.
- Profile of sport (& in particular minority sports) raised.
- eg Women's football 2022 Euros.

## INCREASED MEDIA COVERAGE
- On all sports, but very important for minority sports, eg - table tennis especially in the Olympics.
- May inspire people to try a new activity.
- London 2012 - 5,600 hrs of footage.
- Aired by 500+ TV channels.

## INCREASE IN NATIONAL STATUS
- Eyes of the world on a city/country for duration of Olympics/World Cup.
- Want to look good - no trouble, great facilities, welcoming. Potential future economic benefits.

## IMPROVED NATIONAL MORAL/SOCIAL COHESION
- Unity amongst the population 'want to do well'. Increase in morale, the 'feel good' factor.
- eg Super Saturday London 2012.

## INCREASED DIRECT/INDIRECT TOURISM
- Major Games eg Olympics, put the city/country in the shop window to promote the country's culture & status on the world stage. This may lead to an increase in tourism, either...
- **Direct** - coming to watch games/event at the host city.
- **Indirect** - visiting afterwards or to other parts of the country. Huge economic benefits at local &/or national level.

## IMPROVED SOCIAL INFRASTRUCTURE
- Covers a range of services & facilities meeting strategic & local needs.
- Vital in contributing to a good quality of life.
- Includes... health, education, recreation, sport, play, youth, transport & more
- Money is spent improving facilities/services & the infrastructure in the host city (& beyond sometimes).
- Better facilities for the community & transport links.
- eg London 2012. Transport for London invested £6.5 billion in the transport network
  - 10 rail lines connecting London communities
  - 30 bridges
  - 60 Games related greener travel projects.
- £10 million to upgrade pedestrian & cycle routes.

## INCREASED SHORT TERM EMPLOYMENT
- During the event/games in areas such as hospitality, transport, marketing & coaching (grassroots).
- May continue afterwards.
- eg London 2012 created more than 100,000 jobs, many of which remain still today.

# Potential Negative Aspects During The Event

## Poor Performance by the Home Nation – Impact on Pride/Morale

- This is the reverse effect of the host nation performing well.
- What happens if the team/athletes underperform? May be due to the pressure of being at home?
- Fans will turn, people question why city/country hosted 'legacy' & the negative impact – financial.
- People in the country feel deflated & let down by the athletes.
- May lead to acts of deviance, eg. hooliganism.

## The Potential for Crime and Terrorism
– This is not new!

- Terrorists may see the media coverage as an opportunity to promote their cause. eg. Munich 1972.
- Crime may increase as thieves target fans. eg. muggings. Causes negative publicity & extra security costs.

## An Increase in Transport, Litter & Noise

- Caused by the number of athletes/teams, backroom staff & visitors.
- Qatar is expecting in excess of 1 million fans for the world cup in 2022.
- Impact? Can Games now be Green? Environmental impact must be considered. Recycling facilities?
- Traffic jams for people still working. Idle traffic = increase emissions.

## Perceived Relegation / Lack of Investment

- Whilst the host city/cities benefit from increased media coverage & investment (into facilities & infrastructure), what about the rest of the country?
- Money from taxes used to build stadia, transport links etc comes from whole country. How do they benefit?

## Negative Media Coverage
... of the organisation, infrastructure & facilities.

- The London Olympics in 2012 was covered by 500+ TV stations in 220 territories.
- Coverage is truly global.
- Any issues highlighted will be seen across the world.
- eg. issues at Euro 2020 final at Wembley – organisation & crowd trouble.

- For Beijing 2008, London 2012 & Rio 2016, local people had to move from land/houses used in the construction of venues. Compulsory Purchase Orders used if they refused.
- People have to relocate to other areas.

# Post Event Benefits

Post event/games benefits may be seen by the host city both...
- IMMEDIATELY
- LONG TERM

The long term benefits may be classed as the LEGACY of the Games.

## INCREASE IN SPORTS PARTICIPATION
- If the host does well, people see new role models. eg. Beth Mead, Leah Williamson - England footballers.
- Encourages participation at grassroots level.
- London 2012 - between 2012-2015 400,000 Londoners participated in grass roots sport - the Mayor of London sport legacy programme.

## INCREASE IN PROFILE OF SPORTS
- Involved in the event.
- Links with increase in participation.
- Particularly true for minority sports in Olympics.
- Huge increase in profile of women's football after Euro 2022 & all games covered live on TV. (BBC).

## RAISING THE PROFILE INTERNATIONALLY
- A huge global audience.
- London 2012 had a potential global audience of 4.8 billion, up 0.5 billion compared to Beijing 2008.
- London 2012 received over 60% more broadcast hours than Beijing & double that of Athens 2004.
- If the event goes well, the host's profile is enhanced globally. Impact - potential investment, tourism, £.

## IMPROVED TRANSPORT & SOCIAL INFRASTRUCTURE
- The site of the London 2012 Olympics, London's East End, has been transformed because of the Games.
- The 560 acre site had 4,000 trees planted, parks created, 106 community facilities upgraded, transport links created & developed & still in use today.
- The athletes village was turned into 2818 new homes including 1379 affordable houses.

## IMPROVED/NEW SPORTING FACILITIES
- eg. the Olympic stadium, Aquatics Centre, Velodrome, BMX track, Copper Box, Eton Manor & Riverbank Arena ...but at a cost. All transformed after & still used today. London 2012
- The Commonwealth Games in Birmingham 2022 are renovating & developing existing sites in an effort to leave a carbon neutral legacy.

## INCREASED FUTURE FINANCIAL INVESTMENT
- Links to profile/status.
- Overseas investment more likely to continue if event viewed as a success.

# Post Event Drawbacks

## Loss in National Reputation

- If the event was badly organised
- If the host nation performed badly
- scandals emerge.
- Brazil hosted both the football World Cup & Olympics within 2 years (2014 & 2016), but it didn't run to plan.
- In football, Brazil lost 7-1 to Germany in the semi-final.
- Civil unrest in Brazil, economic decline & corruption.
- Came the Olympics, having spent over $13 billion, some facilities were unfinished.
- The Rio Janeiro state was almost bankrupt!
- 1968 Mexico City Civil Rights protests & Black Power.
- 1972 Munich - Israeli athletes killed by Black September terrorists.
- 1976 Montreal - 22 African countries boycotted due to New Zealand's participation.
- 1980 Moscow - The USA boycotted due to the Soviet invasion of Afghanistan.

## Cost More to Host than Revenue Generated

- Not only is the bidding process expensive, the cost to host is huge!
- The Montreal Olympics in 1976 left debts of $1.3 billion. It was finally paid off in 2006, 30 years later & cost $2.5 billion.
- London 2012 cost £9.5 billion. Costs spiraled from an initial estimate of just over £4 billion.
- The 2004 Athens Olympics cost an estimated $15 billion - huge security costs after 9/11.
- The Rio 2016 Games cost $13.1 billion to host, $3.5 billion over budget.
- The delay to Tokyo 2020/21 cost an extra $2.8 billion, taking the outlay to $15 billion, and no international fans attended.
- The LA Olympics in 1984 were 'LA84' by privately funded by corporate sponsorship, TV rights & private fundraising. Made $232.5 million.

## Sports Facilities Un-Used

- If the event is poorly organised & run, they could be left unused & derelict afterwards.
- eg Athens 2004.
  Beijing 2008.
  Montreal 1976.
- It costs $30 million annually to maintain Sydney's stadium (2000) & $10 million for Beijing's Bird Nest (2008).

# NATIONAL GOVERNING BODIES

## OLYMPIC SPORTS
...such as rowing (British Rowing), cycling (British Cycling) & badminton (Badminton England) receive a lot/most of their funding through **UK Sport** every 4 years, based on their performance at the previous Olympic Games.

## FUNDING
NGBs receive money through the following avenues:
- Sport England funding
- UK Sport funding
- Sponsorship
- TV deals
- Club affiliation fees
- Merchandise & ticket sales

## MEDIA COVERAGE
including TV, radio, newspapers can help drive this through advertising & promotion & the coverage of games. eg. WSL football matches on BBC & Sky.

Inspiring Positive Change run by the FA for women's/girls' football, with the aim to boost numbers playing, volunteering, coaching & international success!

## LOBBY FOR FUNDING
**PROFESSIONAL SPORTS** ...such as football (the FA), rugby union & league (the RFU & RFL) & cricket (the ECB) tend to get most of their funding through TV deals & sponsorship.

## NGBs
- Initially established in the latter years of the 1800s by the 'Old Boys' from the Oxbridge Universities (Oxford & Cambridge) to provide sports with a set of codified laws, rules & regulations.
- Initially developed with the view of recreation - amateur sport.
- Were based on a decentralised system, local associations were self governing.
- However most NGBs are based on a centralised model today where rules, initiatives & policies come from a centralised hub. County & local associations apply them.

## INITIATIVES & POLICIES
- Can be developed to promote & increase participation.
eg. the ECB run All Stars Cricket (aged 5-8) & Dynamos Cricket (aged 8-11) is an 8 week long programme designed for those new to cricket.

## PROMOTE PARTICIPATION
- NGBs want as many people as possible from as many different user groups to play 'their sport - **EQUAL OPPORTUNITIES**.
- focus on developing the participation pyramid. This increases numbers at 'grass roots' up to 'elite' standard.
- How?

# NATIONAL GOVERNING BODIES

## AMEND EXISTING RULES & APPLY DISCIPLINARY PROCEDURES

- Work with NGBs from other countries with regard to rule change proposals.
- eg- 2016 - the ball may be passed forward in football.
- The use of concussion substitutes in football (2021).
- The 50/22 rule in rugby for gaining possession at the lineout (after a kick in own half).
- The NGBs also have disciplinary panels for red cards/offences.
  - eg- the FA gave Richardson a one match ban for throwing flare off the pitch (May 2022).
  - the RFU gave Sean Robinson of Newcastle a 3 week ban for a dangerous tackle (June 2022).
- Referees are the outfield authority in the game.

## PROVIDE SUPPORT, INSURANCE & TECHNICAL GUIDANCE

- To support clubs bidding for funding, sourcing officials or safeguarding issues.
- To keep up to date with rule changes.
- For technical support eg advice regards 3G pitches.
- For insurance issues for the club, players & coaches.

## ORGANISE TOURNAMENTS AND COMPETITIONS

- NGBs organise competitions, leagues & cups.
- eg- the EFL organises fixtures for the Championship, League One & League Two.
- The FA organises the FA Cup from numerous rounds of qualifying through to the final.

## ENSURE SAFETY

- Rules of the game, enforced by the official, attempt to manage game safety.
- If rules are broken, then a player may receive a red/yellow card.
- FA recently banned heading for U12s and below as a trial for the 2022/23 season, due to the link of heading a football and dementia.

## DEVELOP COACHING & OFFICIATING INFRASTRUCTURE

- Coaching & officiating are 2 separate strands of responsibility of an NGB.
- A sport needs coaches to run & develop teams from grassroots upwards.
- Games cannot run without officials.
- Coaching - the FA coaching awards programme...
- Introduction to coaching football. Minimum age 16.
- Uefa C Licence
- Uefa B Licence
- Uefa A Licence in coaching football
- Advanced Youth award
- Uefa Pro Licence
- Plus the 'Respect' module.
- Officiating - the FA Referee course is for ages 14+ to ref mini, 9v9 & 11v11 football.
- Online & face to face sessions.
- 5 online modules including signals, communication, restarts & set pieces.
- 14 hours of face to face training.
- To qualify, you must officiate 5 games. Levels 9 ⇒ 1.

# TECHNOLOGY IN SPORT

Can have both **POSITIVE** & **NEGATIVE** impacts on...
- the **PERFORMER**
- the **SPORT**
- **OFFICIALS**
- **SPECTATORS**

These will be considered over the next 6 pages.

## THE PERFORMER
- Uses technology to **ENHANCE PERFORMANCE**.
- There are lots of examples here.

**METHODS** - can be linked to tracking heart rates (via monitors), running stats (GPS), nutritional analysis to name but a few. More on page ___. Many of these are **wearable tech**.

**EQUIPMENT** - Lighter, bigger, stronger cricket bats, tennis racquets & golf clubs allow balls to be hit harder (sometimes further) & with more control. Ultra light weight carbon fibre cycles/bikes. eg. The Ineos Grenadiers' Tour de France 2022 bike (the Pinarello Dogma F12) weighs just 6.8kg & costs £12,700!!

**CLOTHING** - Base layers, full body swimsuits for swimmers/triathletes, all in one cycling suits, running shoes with carbon fibre plates eg Nike Vaporfly (now banned by World Athletics), light weight football boots, tight fitting clothing in rugby & body armour for protection.

## TECHNOLOGY
for a performer can also help to...

### LOWER THE RISK OF INJURY
- Researchers/technology specialists are developing ever changing tech to make sport safer, including...

**HELMETS** in high contact sports eg American football that release air as a 'shock absorber' when there is an impact.

**MOUTHGUARDS** with LED lights that monitor & assess impact that may lead to a concussion. 'Low impact - blue light' 'Devastating impact - red'

Plus 'basic' safety equipment such as shinpads, appropriate footwear for running, football etc.

### QUICKER RECOVERY FROM INJURY
- Huge recent advances here. See Contemporary Recovery Methods on page 31.

## DISABLED ATHLETES
- There have been huge advances in tech for 'Para Sport' over the past 10-15 years, including...
- Carbon fibre running blades.
- Badminton chairs
- Modified track cycling bikes.
- Release braces for archery.
- Tapping devices for swimmers
- Wheelchair racing chairs & gloves.

26

# TECHNOLOGY IN SPORT

## SPECTATORSHIP
in sport has been hugely impacted by technology.

- Sport can be viewed...
  - **LIVE** in the stadium
  - **AT HOME** watching on TV.

## LIVE
- If you watch games live at the ground, in some sports (eg rugby) you may see replays & reviews of major incidents, such as a review of a high tackle or the grounding of the ball for a try.
- Replays of VAR decisions tend not to happen in football, hence why fans at games do not like it, as they are left 'in the dark' over decisions.
- Some stadia have very large screens, such as the Alexander stadium, venue for the athletics events for the 2022 Commonwealth Games. Here fans could see close up footage of events in 'real time' & 'slow-mo'.

## AT HOME
- The main positives here concern the quality of coverage & the amount/range of games & sports covered.
- Ever improving technology is bringing the audience at home 'ever closer' to the action!

- Games/events can be seen in HD, 4K, 3D and interactively (Red Button).
- There are more games covered, more camera angles, cameras on players (Cricket - the Hundred), cameras on officials (rugby) & on/in equipment (cricket stumps, football goals).
- A huge amount of choice with different channels & broadcasters.
- The internet allows for games/events to be streamed & mobile apps such as 'Sky Go' allow sport to be viewed 'On the go!'.
- Events can be watched from the comfort of your own home.

## HOWEVER... it is not all positive!
- It can be very, very expensive to watch a range of sports via different broadcasters, eg. Sky, Amazon Prime, BT Sport.
- May need specialist equipment.
- 'Armchair' fans may affect numbers at live venues - decrease in revenue for clubs.
- Fibre optic broadband not available everywhere - may be needed for high quality streaming.
- Changes to fixture times, days & even seasons (rugby league) for TV.
- Stop start nature of games now due to VAR, TMO etc.

# TECHNOLOGY IN SPORT

## OFFICIALS

- Much more work has been done recently to help officials in terms of technology.
- Main reasons...

### TO INCREASE FAIR PLAY & INCREASE ACCURACY OF OFFICIATING

- A lot of pressure on officials to make the correct decision. Why? Results ultimately mean $£!!
- e.g.s include...
  - Hawk Eye - Ball tracking used in tennis, cricket & football
  - TMO - Television Match official in rugby union & league
  - VAR - Video Assistant Referee in football.

(More on page 32.)

### MORE ACCURATE DECISIONS

- The use of tech should allow officials to make more accurate decisions & it can be beneficial if used correctly/well.
- However, as can be seen in the Premier League (football), this is not always the case.

- The use of technology 'on the field of play' can also be used by performers if they disagree with a decision by an official. Examples include...
  - Cricket - a player can review a decision if given out/not out.
  - Tennis - a player can review a decision if the ball is deemed out.

## OFFICIALS DECISIONS INFLUENCED BY TECHNOLOGY

- Officials, especially in football now seem to 'dodge' making big decisions. They seem to have become reliant/over reliant on video replays.

- Gets rid of the human error aspect. Is this good or bad?
- Can be vilified or victimised if they get big decisions wrong.

The impact of all these checks is that there is a

## POTENTIAL REDUCTION IN THE FLOW OF THE GAME

- As technology increases & more & more checks take place, this is becoming more of an issue.
- An increased number of stoppages in football to check for offsides & penalties.
- Rugby matches (80 mins) taking over 100 mins due to repeated TMO checks such as the grounding of the ball for a try.

## HOWEVER...

- Not all the impacts of technology on officiating are positive.
- The officials may delay/alter their decisions (referring to video replays - often in slow-mo) & this reduces the flow of the game.

# CONTEMPORARY TECHNOLOGIES

## TRACKMAN
- The trackman machine is becoming increasingly popular in golf, where it can track a shot from 6 foot pitches to 400 yard drives, pinpointing the landing position with an accuracy of less than 1 foot at 100 yards. The shots can be presented in 3D, illustrating the trajectory as well as other parameters in realtime (data can be delivered to electronic devices such as an iPad within a second).
- Examples of key parameters include... swing technique, smash factor, launch angle, ball speed, club head speed, attack angle & club path.

## ADIDAS GMR INSOLES
- This smart insole can track the players' running speed, the power of the kick, touch, control, distance run by the player & the ability to pass the football.
- It is motorised by a Jacquard chip (Google) placed inside the insole of the football boot.

## BAT SENSOR
Bat sensors (Intel-powered Specular or Stancebeam) can be placed at the top of the bat & can measure key elements such as... back lift angle, follow through angle, impact angle, maximum bat speed, bat speed at impact, time to impact, 3D swing & plane path.
- Used to calculate shot timing efficiency & correlate data with hawkeye to see how effective the shot is & how it can be improved.

## GLOBAL POSITIONING SYSTEM - GPS
- Commonly used by elite athletes in team sports during matches & in training. The performance analyst uses the stats to feedback to strength & conditioning coach. Stats included are... metres covered, top sprint speed & heart rate data.
- Data is used to manage player workload & developing areas of weakness.
- Coaches are able to establish player physiological limitations & use the data for basis of making tactical changes during games as stats are now available concurrently.
- More affordable GPS units are now available & are being developed at a fast pace. These can be purchased via the use of a smart watch & can be used for various sports, both on land & in water. eg Skagen Falster 3.

## FITNESS TRACKERS
- Heart rate monitors & pedometers are still used, though the evolution of fitness trackers & smart wrist bands have combined both & added extra data.
- These devices track the HR (though some have stopped this on newer versions to save battery) & also track distance, calories used, steps & monitor sleep.

There are many! Examples here include...

# THE IMPACT OF TECHNOLOGY IN

## HAWKEYE
- Has been revolutionary in both tennis & cricket, where the software follows the trajectory of the ball, allowing for action replays for the fans in the stadia/ground, or the armchair fan at home. eg used when players challenge decisions if given out in cricket, or the ball is called out in tennis.
- Now also used for goal line technology in football (to see if the ball crossed the goal line). Linked to Referee.

## TIMING GATES
- Used in alpine skiing so skiers can track their pace throughout each stage of a race. Allows the viewers at home to do the same.

## RFID CHIPS
- Used to time individuals in long distance races.
- Tiny devices with built in antenna that relay wireless signals.

## TECHNICAL ANALYSIS
- Technological advancements now allow coaches to track & monitor data including HR, running distances, speed & power to tailor training to the individual performer.

## SLOW MOTION CAMERAS
- High definition (HD) cameras are used as photo finish devices in a 100m sprint race, allowing viewers to get a realistic look at the finish.

## SPIDERCAM
- Has been used to show a 'bird's eye' view looking down onto the playing surface.
- Allows viewers to gain an insight into different formations, plays, running lines & fielding positions from another perspective.
eg Spidercam hovering over a football pitch looking downwards to show player movements & formations.

## CAMERAS/MINI-CAMERAS
- Used in many sports & by many officials. Referees use them as part of the review process (VAR). Cameras underwater are used to help adjudicate positions in swimming & the viewers can also follow a performer competing in a BMX race from a helmet-cam.
eg Go Pro.

# CONTEMPORARY RECOVERY METHODS

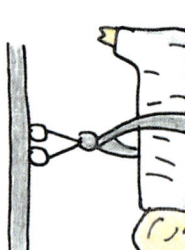

- The following contemporary recovery methods allow for quicker recovery from injury.
- This is a very fluid & ever changing area, with 'new' methods being found & used all the time. Keep your eyes open for changes!

## HYPERBARIC CHAMBERS
- Hyperbaric therapy is a treatment where 100% $O_2$ is administered under pressure greater than the atmospheric pressure.
- This accelerates the recovery of soft tissue micro-tears.

## COMPRESSION CLOTHING
- Increases blood flow to muscles & increased venous return to disperse waste products eg lactic acid.

## HYDROTHERAPY
- Cold water therapy has been proven to reduce muscle soreness & improve recovery times.

## OXYGEN TENT
- Similar to hyperbaric chambers, however $O_2$ tents refer more to supplemental $O_2$ found at normal atmospheric pressure.

## CONTRAST THERAPY
- Hot/cold immersion therapy, placing a limb in warm water, followed by ice cold water. Reduces swelling.

## CRYOTHERAPY
- Involves exposing the body to extremely low temperatures for between 2-4 mins.
- As with ice baths, blood vessels constrict then dilate afterwards, flushing waste products from the body.

## MASSAGE (PHYSIO)
- Widely used as a recovery strategy to reduce muscle soreness & stimulate blood flow.
- Beneficial for prevention & management of injury.

## HYPOXIC TENTS
- Try to simulate high altitude conditions, without having to travel.
- Aims to increase EPO levels/ production (see PEDs)

## ICE BATHS
- Decreases/reduces inflammation & increases recovery rates.
- Blood vessels constrict, then dilate when an athlete gets out.
- Flushes out metabolic waste.

## ULTRASOUND
- Ultrasound waves cause vibration of the tissue (especially those containing collagen).
- Increases muscle temperature, reduces pain & muscle spasms.
- Promotes healing process & blood flow.

# TECHNOLOGY IN SPORT

- As has been seen, there are many, many positive impacts of technology on sport & the performer.
- **HOWEVER**, as has already been said, there are <mark>negative impacts too.</mark>
- These mainly centre around unequal access, cost and availability & affordability.

## INCREASED COST of technological advances.

- This is directly linked to costs.
- Developing 'cutting edge' technology is getting more & more expensive.
- As tech gets more cutting edge, inevitably the cost increased.
- This may mean that not all teams/performers can afford this & so in effect you get an uneven playing field.
- Much of this increase in cost <u>may</u> be covered by sponsors.
- eg- Eliud Kipchoge running a sub 2 hour marathon, sponsored by Ineos & Nike - chemicals, in Nike Vaporfly Next %.

He ran on a specifically chosen course with banked turns, with the help of 41 pace runners. They ran in 5s in a Y shape & followed a laserbeam for the 'ideal' path.

<u>Result</u> - Kipchoge ran 26.2 miles in 1:59.40.2 in Vienna on October 12 2019.

Known as the Ineos 1.59 challenge. All paid by sponsors!

## AVAILABILITY & AFFORDABILITY of technology

- As costs increase, not everyone can afford it.
- This leads to... unequal access.
- This means that increased costs, availability, affordability & unequal access are all linked.
- eg a Hyperbaric Chamber costs up to £23,500 to buy & may cost £30 per hour long session.

In addition to the cost, there may be limited availability in certain areas/countries.

## UNEQUAL ACCESS to the same quality of technology.

- Much will depend on the 'R&D' budget - 'Research & Development' of the team or country.
- Not all performers will have equal access to the same technology.
- Access may depend on location also. Are you near a certain facility?
- It is estimated that Nike have spent over $5billion on research since 2005. This will have a direct <mark>positive</mark> impact on athletes that are sponsored by Nike.

# Extended Answer Questions

## Key Words (blue branch)

**COMMAND**
**TOPIC**
**CONTEXT**

This idea works with all levels of questions

When you look at the question, split it into 3 areas; break it down & highlight KEY WORDS ... basically what is in this guide!

**COMMAND** words tell you how to answer the question.
- Explain
- Discuss
- Describe

are the most commonly used.

**TOPIC** - the subject the answer is based on. eg. role models.

**CONTEXT** - how the topic relate to each other & question. eg. '... the importance of role models.'

## 1 x 8 mark question (purple branch)

There is 1 x 8 mark question at the end of the paper. The content & answers will be relevant & appropriate to Contemporary Issues

## Marking (orange branch)

Answers are marked in levels. Aim for a comprehensive response that is worth 7-8 marks = level 3. It should....

- show detailed knowledge & understanding (not tested in other questions!)
- make many developed points. Linkage is key!
- be well structured with appropriate terminology & relevant examples.
- have minimal (if any) errors (SPaG).

## FAIR! (green branch)

Make your answer FAIR!

- **F - FACT** - state a relevant fact
- **A - APPLY** - this to the question.
- **I - IMPACT** - what is the impact on the topic?
- **R - REPEAT!** 3 or 4 times.